GROVER CLEVELAND

ENCYCLOPEDIA of PRESIDENTS

Grover Cleveland

Twenty-Second and Twenty-Fourth President of the United States

By Zachary Kent

Consultant: Charles Abele, Ph.D.
Social Studies Instructor
Chicago Public School System

CHILDRENS PRESS ®

CHICAGO

The Cleveland family in 1907 (left to right): Esther, Francis, Mrs. Cleveland, Marion, Richard, and Grover

973.8 78??

Ken
11.95

Library of Congress Cataloging-in-Publication Data

Kent, Zachary.
  Grover Cleveland / by Zachary Kent.
    p.   cm. — (Encyclopedia of presidents)
  Includes index.
  Summary: Follows the life of the minister's son who rose from being an honest city lawyer to serve two terms as American president.
  ISBN 0-516-01360-2
  1. Cleveland, Grover, 1837-1908—Juvenile literature.   2.   Presidents—United States—Biography—Juvenile literature.   3.   United States—Politics and government—1885-1889—Juvenile literature.   4.   United States—Politics and government—1893-1897—Juvenile literature.   [1.   Cleveland, Grover, 1837-1908. 2. Presidents.] I. Title. II. Series.
E697.K46   1988
973.8'7'0924—dc19   88-10885
[B]   CIP
[92]   AC

Picture Acknowledgments

AP/Wide World Photos—6, 12, 23, 54, 57, 58, 67, 79 (top), 80 (2 pictures), 84, 86

The Bettmann Archive—62, 85 (bottom)

Historical Pictures Service, Chicago—11, 15, 16, 17, 19, 20, 22, 27, 30, 34, 37 (2 pictures), 38, 44 (2 pictures), 45 (2 pictures), 46, 47, 48, 51, 55, 59, 64, 66, 68, 71 (2 pictures), 73 (top), 74, 77, 79 (bottom), 82 (2 pictures)

Courtesy Library of Congress—4, 5, 39, 50, 52, 60, 61, 73 (bottom), 85 (top), 89

Courtesy U.S. Bureau of Printing and Engraving—2

Cover design and illustration by Steven Gaston Dobson

Childrens Press®, Chicago
Copyright ©1988 by Regensteiner Publishing Enterprises, Inc.
All rights reserved. Published simultaneously in Canada.
Printed in the United States of America.
  2 3 4 5 6 7 8 9 10 R 97 96 95 94 93 92 91 90

Grover Cleveland and
his dog on the porch
of Cleveland's home
in Princeton,
December 6, 1905

Table of Contents

Chapter 1

The Secret aboard the *Oneida*

Panic gripped the United States in 1893. The Philadelphia and Reading Railroad went bankrupt and so did the National Cordage Company. At banks, nervous depositors lined up and withdrew their savings until hundreds of banks were ruined. On Wall Street, stock prices plummeted. Failed businesses closed their doors, leaving more than two million workers walking the streets in search of jobs. At the same time, bad weather spoiled farmers' crops in the South and West.

As the economic depression worsened, worried Americans looked to big, burly, fifty-six-year-old President Grover Cleveland for help and leadership. Cleveland believed the Sherman Silver Purchase Act lay at the root of the problem. This law allowed gold to be drained from the national treasury at an alarming rate. On June 30, 1893, he called for Congress to meet in special session in August. He urged that the Sherman Act be repealed so that "the people may be relieved . . . from present and impending danger and distress."

Tough, stubborn, and completely honest, Grover Cleveland seemed to many citizens the only person with enough political power to change the law. The *Commercial Financial Chronicle* declared, "Mr. Cleveland is about all that stands between this country and absolute disaster." Another magazine, *The Nation*, insisted, "A great deal is staked upon the continuance of a single life."

Americans placed all their faith in Cleveland. They did not realize that at that crucial moment the president faced a personal ordeal of his own. On the same day Cleveland issued his call to Congress, he secretly prepared to undergo a dangerous cancer operation.

A cigar smoker all his life, on June 18, 1893, Cleveland had asked White House doctor Robert M. O'Reilly to look at a sore "rough place" on the roof of his mouth. Doctor O'Reilly discovered an ugly inflamed area the size of a quarter. Further tests soon confirmed that the tissue was cancerous. A specialist, Doctor Joseph D. Bryant, was brought in to examine Cleveland.

"What do you think it is, Doctor?" calmly asked the president.

"Were it in my mouth," gravely answered Bryant, "I would have it removed at once."

In the midst of the nation's worst economic crisis, Cleveland agreed to an operation. He understood, though, that news of his illness would only heighten the fears of Americans who trusted him to remain in charge. Therefore, he insisted upon complete secrecy.

On the afternoon of June 30 Cleveland slipped out of the White House. Along with Doctor Bryant and Secretary of War Daniel Lamont, the president boarded a train bound for New York City. A close friend of Cleveland's, Commodore Elias C. Benedict, agreed to help carry out the secret plan. During the day, trusted crewmen ferried five doctors, an operating table, medical instruments, and other supplies onto Benedict's yacht *Oneida* anchored in New York Bay. By the time Cleveland sneaked aboard that evening, all was ready.

The next day, July 1, the *Oneida* steamed at half-speed up the East River and out into Long Island Sound. As the yacht cut lazily through the glassy water, it gave the outward appearance of a simple pleasure cruise. Below deck, however, the boat's main salon now resembled a floating operating room. Dressed in pajamas, Cleveland climbed heavily into a straight-backed chair that was tied tightly to the mast. Carefully Doctor Ferdinand Hasbrouck, an expert dentist, administered nitrous oxide (laughing gas) to put the patient to sleep. Additional doses of ether kept the president unconscious.

Working quickly, Doctor Hasbrouck pulled two teeth in the region of the cancer. Next, with the patient's mouth stretched open, Doctor Bryant stepped close to the chair to begin the dangerous surgery.

Using a white-hot electric knife and surgical chisels and saws, Bryant cut out a large segment of Cleveland's upper left jawbone. Bryant next sliced through the roof of the president's mouth. In the hollow cavity beyond, the doctor later wrote, he discovered "a soft, gray, gelatinous mass." Cautiously the doctor scooped and scraped out this deadly cancerous matter.

9

Having done as much as possible, the medical team closed the wounds and packed the president's mouth with gauze. In just half an hour the operation was over.

The *Oneida* sailed to Cleveland's seashore vacation home, Gray Gables, in Buzzards Bay, Massachusetts. On July 5, wrapped in a cloak and looking thinner, the president crossed his private dock and entered his house. Newspapermen who lurked about Buzzards Bay could learn only that Cleveland had been treated for two bad teeth. During the next days the president rested.

The operation proved a great success. On July 17 Cleveland underwent a second brief operation on the *Oneida* to scrape the last of the cancer from his mouth. The big man never complained of the terrible pain. While he recuperated, he wrote his important message to Congress. Doctor Kasson C. Gibson fitted the president with an artificial rubber jaw. Cleveland wore the jaw piece inside his cheek and no one could tell he had been ill. His face looked normal and his voice sounded natural.

Although still in discomfort, Cleveland insisted on returning to Washington in August. "The people of the United States are entitled to a sound and stable currency," his message to Congress stated. "Their government has no right to injure them by financial experiment. . . ." With steady courage, Cleveland ignored his own misery and personally fought for repeal of the Sherman Silver Purchase Act. He refused to compromise and on October 30, 1893, Congress finally overturned that law. Two months earlier Doctor Bryant had examined his patient again and happily reported, "All healed."

The New York Stock Exchange during the recession of 1893

Cleveland had scored an incredible double victory. He had beaten the odds against cancer and had survived to win his battle against Congress. The details of Cleveland's heroic operation remained secret until nine years after his death. But Americans already deeply admired the qualities that had propelled Cleveland into the White House as our twenty-second and twenty-fourth president. In a time when crooked, lazy politicians were common, Grover Cleveland remained bluntly firm and hardworking. Above all he was an honest man. "Tell the truth," he always demanded, and it was this sense of fearlessness that rocketed Cleveland from city lawyer to U.S. president in just three short years.

The birthplace of Grover Cleveland in Caldwell, New Jersey

Chapter 2

The Minister's Son

Stephen Grover Cleveland was born on March 18, 1837. His birthplace, a simple but comfortable eight-room house, still stands today at 207 Bloomfield Avenue, Caldwell, New Jersey. The fifth of nine children born to the Reverend Richard Falley Cleveland and Ann Neal Cleveland, the baby was named in honor of local minister Stephen Grover, whose Presbyterian church Reverend Cleveland recently had taken over.

Reverend Cleveland worked hard preparing his Sunday sermons during his time in Caldwell, and little Stephen enjoyed his earliest years in health and loving comfort. He was also blessed with an adventuresome spirit. One day at the age of four he darted into the road in front of his house and fell beneath the wheels of an ox-drawn applecart. Luckily a schoolteacher who was passing by snatched the boy out of danger.

The Cleveland family moved in 1841 when Reverend Cleveland took over another church in Fayetteville, New York. Located near the Erie Canal, this lovely farming village was about eight miles from the city of Syracuse. There Cleveland spent the greatest part of his youth.

Life as the son of a minister was different than that of other boys. Every evening there was a family worship service in the Cleveland house. Stephen memorized passages from the Bible and read classics such as *The Pilgrim's Progress* and Shakespeare's works from the family library. The Clevelands also taught their children solid religious virtues such as the importance of honesty. Later Cleveland explained, "I have always felt that my training as a minister's son has been more valuable to me . . . than any other incident in my life."

Stephen did his share of household chores. He chopped wood, weeded the garden, and baby-sat his younger brothers and sisters. He also took time to have fun. Swimming and fishing were his favorite sports. Later he fondly remembered "old Green Lake and the fish I tried to catch and never did. . . ." In high spirits, he sometimes played pranks at night like ringing the school bell or lifting a neighbor's front gate off its hinges. As he grew larger and stronger, his friends began calling him "Big Steve." As a young adult he preferred to be called Grover.

Cleveland's formal education began at Fayetteville's red frame district schoolhouse. Learning reading, writing, and arithmetic, the youngster was a hardworking student though not a brilliant one. His sister Margaret later recalled, "He was . . . a lad of rather unusual good sense . . . but as a student Grover did not shine." At nine he composed an essay on the importance of spending time well. "If we expect to become great and good men and be respected and esteemed by our friends," he wrote, "we must improve our time when we are young."

The city of Buffalo, New York, at the western end of the Erie Canal

Cleveland used some of his spare time to earn spending money. Near the Erie Canal shippers sometimes needed empty canal boats. For ten cents Cleveland would run to the water's edge and with shouts and waving arms alert passing bargemen.

Money troubles forced Reverend Cleveland to move his family to Clinton, New York, in 1850. For a time the thirteen-year-old boy attended the Clinton Liberal Institute. As district secretary of the American Home Missionary Society, Reverend Cleveland earned $1,000 a year. With so many children, however, he still could not pay all of his bills. To help his family, young Grover quit school at the age of fourteen. John McVicar needed a clerk in his Fayetteville general store. For room, board, and one dollar a week Cleveland was hired on as an apprentice.

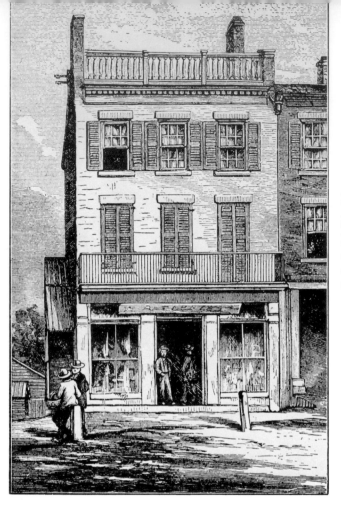

John McVicar's
General Store
in Fayetteville,
New York, where
Grover Cleveland
worked as an
errand boy and
assistant clerk

Cleveland worked long hours in McVicar's store. He shared a barely furnished, unheated room above the store with another young clerk named F. C. Tibbetts. "In winter we fairly froze sometimes," Tibbetts revealed. Well before six o'clock each day Cleveland rose from his cornhusk mattress and hurried downstairs. He swept the store's floor, built a fire, and dusted the shelves. Throughout the day he waited on customers, ran errands, and performed odd jobs. During his second year McVicar raised Grover's pay to two dollars a week. Grover realized, though, that he had no future at McVicar's. When he finished the contract of his apprenticeship, he traveled home to Clinton.

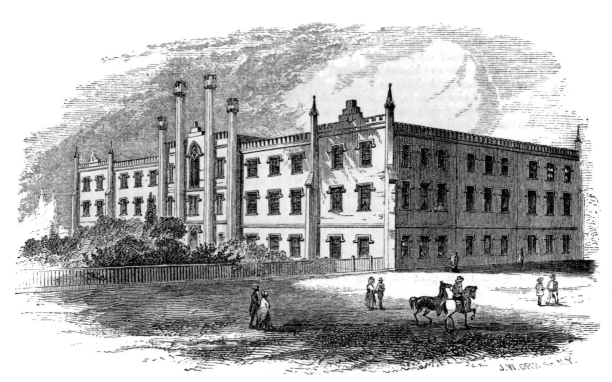

The New York Institution for the Blind

At sixteen Grover was hoping to one day attend Hamilton College located in Clinton. Financial worries, however, forced his father to move the family once again. In 1853 Grover put aside his studies and journeyed with his family to the village of Holland Patent, New York. As minister of the Presbyterian church there, Reverend Cleveland tried to make a success of himself. Years of strain finally overcame the clergyman, however, and he died suddenly on October 1, 1853.

Now more than ever, Grover felt a responsibility to help his mother and younger brothers and sisters. As he watched his father being buried, Grover gave up all hope of attending college. His older brother, William, a teacher at the New York Institution for the Blind, secured a place for Grover as an assistant teacher.

Together the Cleveland brothers made the trip to New York City. At Thirty-Fourth Street and Eighth Avenue they stood before a giant, three-story stone building. The Institution for the Blind took in poor blind children from all over the state and educated them. In 1853, 116 students were attending, ranging in age from twelve to twenty-five. In the school's literary department, Grover taught reading, writing, arithmetic, and geography. At night he helped supervise the boys' dormitory.

Grover soon discovered that life at the institute was very bleak and dreary. In the 1850s the attitude toward disabled people was often cruel and uncaring. T. Colden Cooper, the superintendent of the institute, treated the children as if they were prisoners. Children who broke his strict rules suffered whippings and other punishments. The school's cold, gloomy hallways, bad food, and depressing atmosphere were more than Grover could bear. After a year he quit his job and returned to Holland Patent.

In Holland Patent, Cleveland worried about his future. "I am kind of fooling away my time here," he remarked to his sister Mary. A wealthy local church member, a man named Ingham Townsend, wanted to help the struggling Cleveland family. He offered to pay Grover's way through college if the boy agreed to become a minister. Cleveland turned down that opportunity. He already knew he wanted to travel west and become a lawyer. Instead he accepted a loan from Mr. Townsend for twenty-five dollars with which to make the journey. Years later when he repaid the note he gratefully explained, "The loan you made me was my start in life."

The city of Cleveland from the Reservoir Walk

The rising city of Cleveland, Ohio, attracted the eighteen-year-old's attention because it had been founded by a kinsman, Moses Cleveland. In May 1855, with another Holland Patent boy who also hoped to seek his fortune, Cleveland climbed aboard a train that soon was chugging westward. When the train stopped at the Buffalo, New York, station Cleveland decided to visit his uncle, Lewis F. Allen, who lived in the Black Rock suburb of that city. Lewis Allen was completely surprised to see his nephew and thought his plan to go west, where he knew no one, entirely too risky. "I endeavored to dissuade him," Allen later wrote, "and advised him to remain five months in

Main Street in Buffalo, New York, leading down to the wharf

my employment, where he would be useful." Cleveland
walked back to the railroad station and said good-bye to his
friend, explaining his decision to stay in Buffalo.

The chance visit to his uncle's house changed Grover
Cleveland's life. Among Lewis Allen's business interests
was raising cattle. Carefully he recorded their lines of
breeding in his American Shorthorn herdbook. Now for
room, board, and ten dollars a month Cleveland penned
the numbers and other information into this ledger. More
importantly, at the end of five months Lewis Allen
obtained a position for Cleveland with a Buffalo law firm.

Working as a clerk at the office of Rodgers, Bowen and Rodgers, Cleveland would receive four dollars a week while he studied law.

During his first day there, old Henry W. Rodgers tossed a copy of *Blackstone's Law Commentaries* on Cleveland's desk with a thud. "That's where they all begin," he simply commented. As they scurried about the office, workers ignored Cleveland as he studied. At lunchtime they forgot he was there and accidentally left him locked inside. "Some day I will be better remembered," the young clerk grimly told himself. On another day his uncle asked him how he was getting along. "Pretty well, sir," replied Cleveland, "only they won't tell me anything." When Rodgers learned of this remark he flatly told Allen, "If the boy has brains, he will find out for himself."

Cleveland studied hard, poring over books in the office law library. He watched the firm's other clerks prepare legal documents. He listened when the firm's partners discussed cases. Gradually, in this haphazard manner, he learned the law profession. In time Cleveland's steady work habits gained attention. "My employers assure me," he wrote home early in 1857, "that if I keep on I'll make a lawyer."

Cleveland finally reached his goal in May 1859, when the New York State supreme court admitted him to the bar. Rodgers, Bowen and Rodgers immediately offered the new twenty-two-year-old lawyer a job with the firm. Earning $1,000 a year, Cleveland was better able to help his family. Every month he folded some money into an envelope and mailed it to his mother in Holland Patent.

Boats and factories of the industrious city of Buffalo

The Allen family felt slighted when Cleveland gave up
his room at their lovely Black Rock home. The independent young lawyer, however, wished to be close to the
office in downtown Buffalo. During the next years he
lived in cheap boardinghouses and hotels. Most often,
though, he could be found bent over his desk late at night
scribbling legal papers.

Buffalo in 1860 offered a lawyer many opportunities for
work. In just ten years the city had doubled in size to
81,000 people. Located on the shores of Lake Erie near the
mouth of the Erie Canal, Buffalo boasted a busy harbor.
Along the waterfront swarms of laborers loaded and
unloaded boats heading east and west. With smoking

Immigrants arriving in New York City in the early 1890s

chimneys, the city's thriving iron foundries, mills, factories, and breweries attracted eager new workers to Buffalo every day.

The rapid growth of Buffalo's industry and population was typical of many northern cities in the United States. Every day thousands of European immigrants were pouring into the country willing to do factory work for low wages. Across the North railroad lines were being built, and steam locomotives roared across the countryside carrying produce from one city to another. In the southern states, however, cotton remained the major crop. Southern plantation owners depended on black slaves for the success of their farming economy.

Many people believed slavery was cruel, and one group of northerners called abolitionists demanded that it be ended. Rather than submit to pressure, in 1861 eleven southern states quit the Union and formed the Confederate States of America. In April 1861 the American Civil War erupted when Confederate cannon fired on the Union garrison at Fort Sumter in Charleston, South Carolina.

Throughout the North patriotic young men quickly joined the Union army and vowed to fight to keep the North and South together as one nation. Cleveland met with his younger brothers, Fred and Cecil, in the spring of 1861. Together they agreed that Fred and Cecil would volunteer for army service while Grover continued working to support their mother and needy sisters. While cannon roared and muskets cracked on battlefields far away, Cleveland labored harder than ever to assist his family with money.

Democratic politics had interested Cleveland since his arrival in Buffalo. During elections he tramped the streets reminding Democrats to vote. By 1862 he was elected Democratic supervisor of his city ward. Local Democratic leaders took notice of Cleveland's party loyalty and organizing skills. That same year they appointed him assistant district attorney for Erie County.

The Buffalo *Courier* soon announced, "Mr. Cleveland is one of the most promising of the younger members of the bar, is a thoroughly read lawyer, and possesses talent of a high order." In his new position Cleveland handled several important lawsuits and more than once conducted four cases in a single day.

Sadly, the Civil War still raged in 1863. To raise more troops to fight for the North, the U.S. Congress passed a draft law on March 3. During the first drawing Cleveland discovered he was drafted. The draft law allowed him to find a substitute to serve in his place. Having just finished his term of service, his brother, Fred, offered to reenlist. Cleveland, however, replied, "Fred has done enough. I have my man."

For $150 Cleveland hired a Polish immigrant named George Benninsky as his substitute. Benninsky served in the army until the end of the war. At the same time Cleveland continued his work in Buffalo as the county's assistant district attorney.

Just after April 9, 1865, people cheered and danced in the streets of Buffalo. Confederate general Robert E. Lee had surrendered his army to Union general Ulysses S. Grant at Appomattox Court House, Virginia. The Confederacy had collapsed. The United States were once again reunited and slavery was abolished.

As the nation returned to peace, twenty-eight-year-old Cleveland attempted to win the position of Erie County district attorney. The Buffalo *Courier* supported his candidacy. "He is a young man," it claimed, "who, by his unaided exertions, has gained a high position at the bar, and whose character is above reproach."

In the fall election, however, Cleveland lost to his close friend Lyman K. Bass. In political defeat, he returned to private law practice. Taking on three different partners in six years, Cleveland's reputation as a lawyer continued to rise.

Not until 1870 did Cleveland run for public office again. "Grover Cleveland, the candidate for sheriff," the Buffalo *Courier* praised him, "is perhaps the most popular man in the Democratic party of the county. . . . He will . . . make one of the best sheriffs Erie County ever had." By a slim margin of 303, voters elected Cleveland to the demanding position of sheriff. Many people considered the job an undignified step backward in Cleveland's career. His greatest duty was the running of the county jail. The work paid very well, however, and Cleveland's truthful character brought honor to the office.

Tough sailors roamed Buffalo's waterfront in the early 1870s. Workingmen squandered their pay in dozens of gambling houses and saloons. Fights, robberies, and other crimes kept the jail quite busy. Cleveland discovered that the political leaders who supplied the jail with food and fuel often cheated on deliveries. The thirty-three-year-old sheriff angrily exposed such thievery and thereafter personally counted sacks of flour and oatmeal and measured cords of wood when they arrived. Cleveland would not tolerate dishonesty of any kind.

One of Cleveland's unpleasant tasks as sheriff was to serve as the county hangman. In 1872 a man named Patrick Morrissey had murdered his mother and was sentenced to die. At high noon on September 6 Morrissey stood on the execution platform and Cleveland personally dropped the trap. In 1873 another man, Jack Gaffney, killed an enemy in a quarrel. As a result of his trial Gaffney also was condemned to death. On the day of execution Sheriff Cleveland again stepped forward and

Scenes of Buffalo, New York, in 1878

performed his grim duty as hangman. Although he could have paid a jailer to do these hangings, Cleveland refused to shirk his responsibility, no matter how disagreeable.

When his term as sheriff ended in 1873, Cleveland returned to his law career. Slowly his reputation as a lawyer grew. Other attorneys marveled at his energy and physical strength. Sometimes he worked all night on an important case. At dawn he turned off his gas lamp, quickly bathed, drank a cup of hot coffee, and hurried off to court.

Every case he undertook, he prepared very carefully. In court he displayed an excellent memory, often speaking without notes. "He was a good jury lawyer and frequently became eloquent before juries," Judge Edward Hatch later remembered. "His great strength was his candor, his thorough integrity . . . they gave him a standing and insured him a respectful hearing at all times."

Throughout the 1870s Cleveland enjoyed his rising success and personal independence. Still a bachelor, Cleveland kept an apartment in the business section of the city. In his free time he visited neighborhood saloons where he played cards and checkers. Buffalo possessed a large German population. From dozens of local German-style beer gardens, the music of brass bands and loud singing wafted through the air. Happily seated with laborers and merchants, Cleveland drank steins of beer and consumed plates of sauerkraut and sausages, thick stews, and sweet desserts. For exercise Cleveland sometimes vacationed in the New York countryside. Beside lakes and streams he loved to fish for bass and trout. In the woods he sometimes stalked deer with a favorite rifle he affectionately called "Death and Destruction." Years of hearty eating, though, gradually changed his appearance.

Standing five feet eleven inches tall, by 1880 Cleveland weighed over 250 pounds. A giant, hulking figure, his broad shoulders, thick chest, and muscular arms easily filled his coat. His brown hair was thinning and he wore a bushy mustache. His head was large and his double chin hung over his collar. But his twinkling blue eyes revealed his energy and his big fists showed his strength. One day in a barroom argument over politics, Cleveland lost his temper with a man named Mike Falvey. A witness later remembered, ". . . whatever the start may have been, the finish began when Falvey called Cleveland a liar. Cleveland banged him into the gutter near Seneca Street."

But the burly lawyer could behave like a gentleman, too. In 1877 Cleveland helped found the exclusive City Club in Buffalo. Sometimes for relaxation he visited there neatly dressed and wearing a top hat.

Cleveland got along well with children. His many nieces and nephews called him "Uncle Jumbo." Young Cleveland Bacon never forgot a visit to his uncle's apartment. There he saw deep easy chairs and tables with books and cigars strewn across them. When he asked what his uncle kept in his icebox, Cleveland smiled and replied, "Watermelons!"

One of Cleveland's dearest friends was fellow lawyer Oscar Folsom. In 1864 Folsom's little girl, Frances, was born. Cleveland went to see the pretty baby and later bought her a baby carriage. Sadly, in 1875, Oscar Folsom died in a buggy accident. The court appointed Cleveland the administrator of Folsom's estate. Thereafter he watched over the Widow Folsom's business affairs and became legal guardian to eleven-year-old "Frankie." Through the next years he took a special interest in the child's upbringing. As he entered middle age, Cleveland's sisters sometimes pestered him about his bachelor lifestyle and told him he should get married. In answer, the giant man teased, "I'm only waiting for my wife to grow up." Neither he nor Frances Folsom could have guessed how true his statement was.

Chapter 3

The Veto Politician

Crooked politicians had controlled the city government of Buffalo for many years. These "bosses" accepted bribes from city contractors, rigged elections, and grafted money from the city treasury. By 1881 the decent citizens of Buffalo refused to put up with this corruption any longer. They were determined to find an honest man to run for mayor. Several possible candidates declined to run when asked. Finally the reformers thought of Grover Cleveland.

Through hard work and reliability, Cleveland had made himself one of the city's most respected lawyers. Even more important, the former sheriff had a reputation for being "ugly honest." He hated the bosses and seemed just the kind of man the city needed.

In October 1881, a committee of three men went looking for Cleveland and found him busy with a trial in court. "The Committee," recalled Judge Albert Haight, "came into court and attracted the attention of Cleveland, who stepped aside and held a brief conference. Then he came up to my desk, leaning his elbows on it, and talking across in low tones.

Opposite page: Cleveland as victorious governor over the Democratic "bosses"

" 'This,' he said, indicating the committee with a nod, 'is a committee from the Democratic convention, and they want to nominate me for Mayor. They've come over to see if I'll accept. What shall I do about it?' "

"I think you had better accept," the judge replied.

"But I'm practising law and don't want it interfered with," objected Cleveland.

"The Mayoralty is an honorable position," urged Judge Haight. "We are all interested in having a good city government. You're an old bachelor. You haven't any family to take care of. I'd advise you to accept."

Later that day a committeeman rushed into Buffalo's Democratic headquarters. "He's accepted, boys! He's accepted!" the man shouted. "Let's have a drink!"

During his tough campaign the forty-four-year-old mayoral candidate pledged to bring honesty and efficiency into the government. "Why," he declared, "should not public interests be conducted in the same excellent manner as private interests?" By a vote of 15,120 to 11,528, the people of Buffalo agreed and elected him their mayor.

As soon as he took office on January 1, 1882, Mayor Cleveland warned city employees that they had to give a full day's work or risk being fired. He set an example by working hard himself, until soon he became known as the "Veto Mayor." When corrupt city councilmen tried to pass laws that wasted money, Cleveland promptly turned them down with his veto power. He vetoed bills for unnecessary sidewalks and needless printing costs. He vetoed small gifts to friends of politicians and refused to let government workers charge the city for personal expenses.

Cleveland demanded that city contracts be awarded fairly, too, and in the spring of 1882 he made his greatest impact yet. Dishonest councilmen wished to give the Buffalo street-cleaning contract to the highest bidder in exchange for bribes. Other companies offered to do the work for much less money. Angrily Cleveland vetoed the bill. "I withhold my consent," he exclaimed, ". . . because I regard it as [a] . . . shameless scheme to betray the interests of the people, and to worse than squander the public money." The citizens of Buffalo roundly applauded Cleveland's honesty.

Mayor Cleveland also showed common sense in dealing with the city's sewage problem. Sewage festering in a local canal and seeping into wells for drinking water caused typhoid fever and other diseases that killed over 1,300 Buffalo residents in 1881.

Cleveland demanded that the danger be corrected at once. He turned down council efforts to set up an expensive commission of local politicians to investigate the problem. Instead he insisted on hiring knowledgeable engineers who were not on the city payroll to close filthy wells and clean up the unhealthy mess. "I believe that the poor," he announced, "should . . . have access . . . to . . . pure and wholesome water."

Cleveland continued to attack crookedness wherever he saw it in city government. Through honest, effective leadership the veto mayor saved the city one million dollars in less than a year. Before the end of summer 1882, the Buffalo *Sunday Times* openly suggested Cleveland would make an excellent governor.

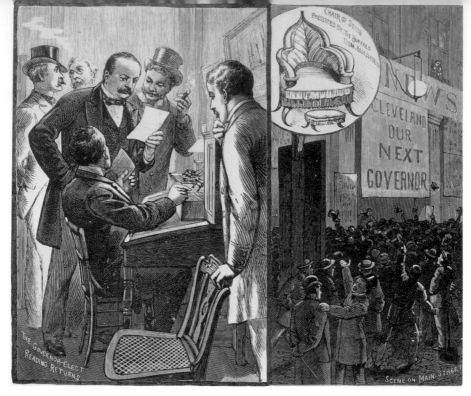

Election day, November 1882

Corrupt politicians, especially the bosses of Tammany
Hall in New York City, controlled the state government the
same way the dishonest councilmen of Buffalo had controlled that city. Impressed by Cleveland's stubborn
courage, New York's reform Democrats now called for
Cleveland's nomination as governor. Although Cleveland
was unknown outside western New York, at the state convention in September 1882 Democrats cheered his spirit of
independence and nominated him to run. Honest citizens
throughout the state supported Cleveland. Even the bosses
who lounged at Tammany Hall promised to vote for him.
Unfamiliar with Cleveland, they believed they could control him after the election. New Yorkers who demanded a
change lined up at polling places on election day that
November. By a landslide margin of nearly 200,000 votes,
Cleveland beat Charles J. Folger, his Republican opponent.

Cleveland understood his tremendous challenge. To his brother, William, he wrote hopefully, "I know that I am honest and sincere in the desire to do well, but the question is whether I know enough to accomplish what I desire." To a visitor at his office he confided, "Let me rise or fall, I am going to work for the interests of the people of the State, regardless of party or anything else."

Cleveland arrived at Albany, the state capital, in clear, cold weather. On January 1, 1883, he took the oath of office and delivered a ringing speech without using notes. Vigorously the new governor took up his duties. Often he worked long hours at the capitol, arriving early and staying long after dark. One night after working until eleven o'clock Cleveland joked to his secretary, "Well, I guess we'll quit and call it half a day."

The doors of his office were always open. He kept nothing secret and allowed anyone to visit him. Office-seekers often crowded around his desk hoping to obtain government positions. Cleveland examined all applications carefully and only awarded jobs to deserving, qualified people. When office-seekers whispered requests for favors, the blunt governor often answered them in a loud voice that everyone in the room could hear. One day a Democratic job applicant complained, "Don't I deserve it for my party work?" Cleveland answered, "I don't know that I understand you," and stared at him coldly until the man sheepishly left the office. The governor's forthright behavior stunned crooked members of the New York legislature who had expected to fill many government jobs with their friends.

Long hours and tireless personal industry allowed the governor to read every word of every piece of legislation that crossed his desk. Again and again the outraged bosses of Tammany Hall learned that Cleveland had turned down dishonest bills they hoped would pass. Soon the "Veto Mayor" came to be known as the "Veto Governor."

"The State should not only be strictly just," Cleveland let people know, "but scrupulously fair." When the Five Cent Fare bill reached his desk, Cleveland revealed how completely fair he intended to be. The hated New York millionaire Jay Gould, who controlled the New York City elevated railroad system, charged passengers ten cents during certain hours of the day. Reform legislators declared the fare was too high and passed a law lowering it to five cents. The people of New York City loudly approved and demanded that Cleveland sign the bill into law. Careful study of the measure, however, showed Cleveland that, according to Gould's legal contract, it would be against the law to lower the fare. Therefore he vetoed the bill and awaited the public outcry. "By tomorrow at this time," he remarked after turning it down, "I shall be the most unpopular man in the State of New York." Surprisingly, the people accepted the logic of Cleveland's stand.

In two years' time, Cleveland's stubborn sense of fairness earned him the nickname "His Obstinacy." He passed bills to enlarge the state's water supply and establish a 1.5-million-acre park at Niagara Falls. His many vetoes of corrupt bills won him the bitter hatred of Tammany Hall leaders. But the common citizens happily began to describe their governor as "Grover the Good."

Above: The New York State capitol building in Albany
Below: An 1883 cartoon of Cleveland, the "Veto Governor"

Torchlight procession in honor of Cleveland's presidential nomination

The city of Chicago came alive in July 1884 as Democratic delegates arrived for their national convention. Huddled together at hotel room meetings, these politicians discussed who would make the strongest presidential candidate. Grover Cleveland's success as mayor and governor impressed many of these men. One angry delegate from Tammany Hall responded to this talk by declaring, "Cleveland cannot carry the state of New York."

Most Democrats, however, were tired of Tammany's greed and scheming practices. When the convention opened, Cleveland's name was quickly offered for nomination. In a seconding speech, the Wisconsin delegate rose and spoke for the people of his state. "They love him, gentlemen," he said of Cleveland, "and they respect him,

A Cleveland-Hendricks campaign poster

not only for himself, for his character, for his integrity and judgment and iron will, but they love him most of all for the enemies he has made."

On the second ballot Grover Cleveland won the Democratic nomination for president. To run for vice-president the Democrats chose Thomas Hendricks of Indiana. As the news spread, New Yorkers joyously celebrated. In Albany, as usual, Governor Cleveland could be found laboring over his desk when the sound of distant cannon echoed through the windows. "They are firing a salute, Governor, for your nomination," remarked one of his assistants. "That's what it is," exclaimed another, listening. Cleveland paused and wondered, "Do you think so? Well, anyhow we'll finish up this work."

Many newspapers across the country thought Cleveland the best possible choice for president. The *New York World* explained its reasons for supporting Cleveland:

"1. He is an honest man; 2. He is an honest man; 3. He is an honest man; 4. He is an honest man."

Campaign worker William C. Hudson hurriedly created a slogan for the upcoming race. "Public Office is a Public Trust," he quoted Cleveland as saying.

"Where the deuce did I say that?" asked the governor doubtfully.

"You've said it a dozen times publicly, but not in those few words," answered Hudson.

"That's so," agreed Cleveland. "That's what I believe. I'll stand for it and make it my own."

To oppose Cleveland, the Republican party picked former Maine congressman James G. Blaine. A brilliant politician and national leader, Blaine was highly respected by many. Loyal Republicans said he possessed a "magnetic" personality because of his gentle manners and tremendous charm. They dubbed Blaine with the nickname "The Plumed Knight."

Some independent Republicans, however, referred to Blaine as "Slippery Jim." They claimed that Blaine was power hungry, lacking in scruples, and even dishonest. The *New York Sun* dismissed this faction of unhappy Republicans by teasingly calling them "Mugwumps" (an Algonquin Indian word meaning "chief"). In a search for honest, reform government, the Mugwumps bolted from the Republican ranks, and many of them agreed to support Grover Cleveland.

Voters who hated Blaine accused him of accepting a bribe of one hundred thousand dollars from a railroad while serving as Speaker of the House of Representatives. They claimed that Blaine then used his influence in Congress to help the railroad. One secret note Blaine wrote to a railroad official at that time contained the warning "Burn this letter." This embarrassing letter reappeared in newspapers in 1884 and caused grinning Democrats and Mugwump campaigners to chant "Burn this letter! Burn this letter! Burn, burn, oh burn this letter!"

Within days, though, on its front page, the *Buffalo Evening Telegraph* revealed an even more explosive scandal involving Cleveland. "A TERRIBLE TALE," blared the banner headline, "A DARK CHAPTER IN A PUBLIC MAN'S HISTORY." The story declared that in 1874 Cleveland had had a romantic relationship with a young Buffalo widow named Maria Halpin. Mrs. Halpin later claimed Cleveland was the father of her baby boy.

As details of the story became known, loyal Democrats hurried to Cleveland's defense. One report in the *New York World* explained that, as a young man, Cleveland "met this woman . . . and became intimate with her. She was a widow, and not a good woman by any means. Mr. Cleveland, learning this, began to make inquiries about her, and discovered that two of his friends were intimate with her at the same time as himself. When a child was born, Cleveland, in order to shield his two friends, who were both married men, assumed responsibility of it." Until the little boy later was adopted legally into a good family, Cleveland paid for his support.

No presidential candidate ever had suffered such a personal scandal. Many upright Americans condemned Cleveland for his behavior. Friends tried to persuade Cleveland to deny it ever happened. Cleveland never hesitated, however. With regard to the Halpin affair he courageously announced, "Above all, tell the truth." He refused to hide this embarrassment from his past.

One day a Democrat entered the governor's office and presented Cleveland with documents attacking Blaine's private life and character, too. Cleveland thanked the man and paid for the papers. Then he tore them into little pieces and ordered them burned in the fireplace. To his astonished secretary he firmly stated, "The other side can have a monopoly of all the dirt in this campaign."

In truth, with both candidates the victims of scandals, the United States in 1884 had never witnessed such a dirty campaign. In torchlight marches Democrats chanted:

"Blaine! Blaine! James G. Blaine!
The Continental liar from the State of Maine!"

In answer, parading Republicans loudly attacked Cleveland by yelling:

"Ma, ma, where's my Pa?
Gone to the White House, ha, ha, ha!"

"The public is angry and abusive," revealed author Henry Adams in a letter. "We are all swearing at each other like demons." The *Nation* sadly reported on October 23, "Party contests have never before reached so low a depth of degradation in this . . . country."

Through the summer and fall the ugly fight continued. Although Cleveland's hope of winning dwindled, he remained in Albany hard at work as governor instead of actively campaigning. Blaine, on the other hand, made a whirlwind tour across the nation. Confident of victory, Blaine visited New York at the end of October in an effort to win additional votes in that crucial state. At a public rally of ministers, Blaine quietly listened as the Reverend Samuel D. Burchard declared, "We are Republicans, and don't propose to leave our party and identify ourselves with the party whose [forerunners] have been rum, Romanism, and rebellion." Blaine seemed to support this statement, which insulted members of the Roman Catholic religion, many of whom lived in the large industrial cities of the northeast.

Later in the day Blaine made a second grave mistake when he attended an expensive dinner paid for by millionaire Jay Gould. Common people resented Blaine's association with the rich. The *New York World* angrily reported the event with the headlines: "THE ROYAL FEAST OF BELSHAZZAR BLAINE AND THE MONEY KINGS . . . AN OCCASION FOR THE COLLECTION OF A REPUBLICAN CORRUPTION FUND."

Overnight thousands of Roman Catholics, especially the Irish in New York, turned against Blaine. Many workingmen also decided they preferred Cleveland's simple honesty rather than Blaine's shady friendships with the wealthy class. Just five days before the election, the contest between Cleveland and Blaine suddenly became too close to predict.

Above: A Republican attack on Cleveland's Maria Halpin scandal
Below: The rally where Burchard spoke of "rum, Romanism, and rebellion"

Right: A cartoon showing Cleveland faithfully attending to his duties in spite of temptations

Below: An admission ticket to the 1884 Democratic national convention

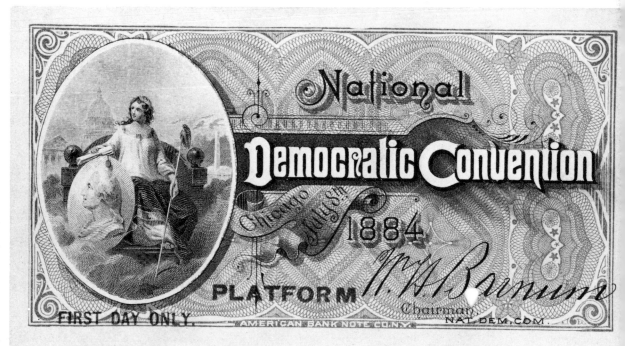

An October 1884 rally for Cleveland in Buffalo, New York

Cleveland still believed he had no chance to win. On election day, November 4, 1884, the governor voted in Buffalo. Then in an icy rain he traveled by train to Albany to await results. The election proved so close that for three days it was uncertain who had won. When the votes finally were tallied, Cleveland learned he had carried the important state of New York by a bare 1,149 votes out of more than 1,100,000 cast. A count of votes nationwide revealed:

	Popular Vote	Electoral Vote
Grover Cleveland	4,911,017	219
James G. Blaine	4,848,334	182

President Grover Cleveland

A slim margin of less than 63,000 votes had elected Grover Cleveland president of the United States. In just three years, Americans had lifted Cleveland from city lawyer to the highest public office in the land. In spite of his personal scandal, the people chose Cleveland rather than Blaine. Still the embarrassment of the dirty 1884 campaign left Cleveland feeling deeply wounded. As duty called him to Washington, Cleveland revealed to a friend, "I look upon the four years next to come as a . . . self-inflicted penance for the good of my country. I can see no pleasure in it and no satisfaction, only a hope that I may be of service to my people."

Chapter 4

The Veto President

Bright sunshine sparkled through the sky on the freezing day of March 4, 1885, in Washington, D.C. At the White House, forty-seven-year-old Grover Cleveland climbed into an open carriage with President Chester A. Arthur. Four bay horses drew the coach past cheering crowds along Pennsylvania Avenue.

An even larger crowd awaited the inauguration ceremony on the grounds of the Capitol. At noon Cleveland's great, bulky figure stepped out onto the platform erected on the Capitol's east portico. With his hand upon an open Bible he took the oath of office, vowing to "preserve, protect and defend" the laws of the Constitution. Then he turned and delivered his inaugural address from memory.

"The people demand reform in the administration of the government," his loud, vibrant voice echoed over the listening throng. As Cleveland prepared to begin his duties as twenty-second president of the United States, many Americans believed they had elected just the man to undertake that job.

Opposite page: A drawing meant to demonstrate
the meaning of Cleveland's election

The inauguration of President Grover Cleveland in 1885

The bachelor president put himself to work with customary energy. Before nine o'clock each morning Cleveland pulled back his chair and sat down at his White House desk. Through the day he answered letters, talked to congressmen and government officials, and sometimes simply shook hands with lines of visitors who came to wish him well. On Tuesdays and Thursdays the department heads who served as Cleveland's cabinet filed into the White House for meetings with the president. Through the afternoons, evenings, and late into the nights Cleveland could be found still laboring at his desk.

**Miss Rose Elizabeth Cleveland,
the president's sister and White House hostess**

Washington citizens sometimes spied the president taking a morning stroll or an afternoon carriage ride. With such limited free time, it was the only exercise he allowed himself. At mealtimes the White House cook served fancy dishes of rich foods. Often Cleveland longed for simpler things to eat. "I must go to dinner," he once wrote a friend. "I wish it was to eat a pickled herring, Swiss cheese and a chop . . . instead of the French stuff I shall find." To serve as hostess at official White House dinners, the unmarried president invited his sister Rose to live with him. A former private schoolteacher, Miss Cleveland filled the White House with a sense of dignity and culture.

Cleveland was plagued by many visitors to his office.

During the early days of Cleveland's term, thousands of joyful Democrats flocked to Washington. No Democrat had been elected president since 1856, and for years American politicians had believed in the saying, "To the victors belong the spoils." Now Democratic spoilsmen lined up at the White House demanding federal jobs ranging from village postmaster to ambassador. "The clock has just struck ten," Cleveland wrote to a friend one morning, "and the doors must be opened to the waiting throng. The question with me is, When (if ever) will this thing stop?"

Insisting that the federal positions within his power be filled only with qualified people, Cleveland dealt with this steady stream of office-seekers bluntly.

One day he cut a job hunter short by roughly saying, "Why, I was not aware that there was a vacancy in that position." Another man he turned away remarked, "If you see him once and look at that face and jaw, you will believe he means what he says."

Still, day after day these Democratic office-seekers tormented him.

"This dreadful, frightful . . . office seeking hangs over me and surrounds me," he finally complained. In the end he replaced 80,000 federal employees. However, he protected the jobs of some 40,000 others with broadened civil service laws.

Over the years many government offices had ballooned in size. In an attempt to save the government money, Cleveland trimmed unnecessary workers from department staffs.

At the Land Office he discovered several injustices, which he promptly corrected. Unfair land grants to powerful railroads in the West prevented homesteaders from settling on thousands of acres of land. Cleveland recovered much of this property and opened it to the public.

Other lands in the Oklahoma and Dakota territories were being stolen from peaceful Indians and given to land speculators. Cleveland canceled the opening of these vast plains, returned ownership of the land to the Indian reservations, and threatened to use federal troops to keep land grabbers away.

Geronimo, Apache warrior and chief

In the Southwest, Cleveland ordered U.S. soldiers to capture renegade Indians. After years of unfair treatment, a band of Apaches led by the famous chief Geronimo escaped for a second time from their reservation. For months these Apaches rampaged across the deserts and mountains of the Arizona-New Mexico region raiding settlements. Blue-clad cavalrymen cornered these fierce warriors in August 1886 and forced them to surrender.

Apaches Natchez and Geronimo, captured by federal troops

While frontiersmen conquered the last of the American West, the rest of the nation rumbled with financial and labor worries. For years the government had protected American industry by placing high import taxes on many foreign products. These taxes, collectively known as the tariff, filled the U.S. Treasury with a huge surplus. As the money piled higher, congressmen proposed spending it on wasteful and sometimes dishonest government projects. These attempts angered Cleveland. He realized the high tariff would cause a trade imbalance in the long run and upset the nation's economy by destroying competition.

No president ever had devoted an entire annual message to a single subject. In December 1887, though, Cleveland addressed Congress on the tariff and nothing else. Forcefully he argued that the current tariff was a "betrayal of American fairness and justice." He called for the lowering of import taxes. Cleveland knew beforehand that his speech would anger many powerful people, but he insisted, "What is the use of being elected or re-elected unless you stand for something?"

While the tariff issue raged, American corporations and their owners continued to reap enormous profits. Their workers, however, experienced no such luck. Forced to work long hours in dark, dreary, unsafe, and unhealthy sweatshops and factories, America's laborers struggled to overcome misery. Cleveland observed the overall problem with growing concern. In a speech to Congress he complained that "wealth and luxury" existed in America beside "poverty and wretchedness. . . . The gulf between employers and the employed is constantly widening."

Over the years unhappy workers began to band together and form trade unions. Union members increasingly threw down their tools and went on strike. On picket lines and at protest rallies these laborers refused to return to their jobs until their demands were met. In 1886, for example, hundreds of railroad strikes flared up across the nation as the new Knights of Labor union demanded higher wages and an eight-hour workday for its members.

The wealthy class angrily resisted making changes in their businesses. Rather than give in, they often fired their workers altogether or hired thugs to break up strikes.

Chicago police try to control mobs during the Haymarket Riot.

Some of the most radical members of the working class became revolutionaries. These "anarchists" called for the complete destruction of the government. On May 4, 1886, anarchists addressed some 1,300 striking factory workers at a rally in Haymarket Square in Chicago. One hundred eighty policemen stood on hand to break up the meeting at the slightest sign of violence. Suddenly someone tossed a bomb among these policemen. Its roaring explosion killed seven officers and injured fifty others. Screams and gunshots erupted as horrified people fled the scene. In the days following the tragic incident, many fearful Americans turned against the trade unions. Even today the Haymarket Riot is remembered as a black chapter in the history of America's labor movement.

Frances Folsom Cleveland

While rich and poor Americans grappled with their class differences, in the spring of 1886 a startling development in President Cleveland's personal life captured everyone's attention. For years Cleveland had watched the progress of his ward, Frances Folsom, with interest. Although he did not realize it, he had indeed been waiting for her to grow up. By the time she graduated from Wells College in 1885, she had grown into a lovely and well-mannered young woman. In spite of the difference in their ages, Cleveland fell in love with her. A romance soon blossomed between them, and when he proposed marriage, she accepted.

The sudden announcement of Cleveland's wedding plans completely surprised Washington society. The tenth

Grover and Frances are married in the White House, June 2, 1886.

U.S. president, John Tyler, had remarried while he was president, but no president ever had been married inside the White House itself. On June 2, 1886, thousands of excited and curious citizens jammed the White House lawn. Inside the mansion, close friends and family gathered in the Blue Room to witness the happy ceremony. John Philip Sousa directed the Marine Corps Band to play the wedding march as the forty-nine-year-old groom entered with his twenty-one-year-old bride. The Reverend Byron Sunderland performed the service, in which President Cleveland and Miss Folsom vowed to "love, honor, and . . . keep" one another. As the ceremony concluded, church bells throughout the district joyfully rang and twenty-one guns in Navy Yard thundered a rousing salute.

Oak View, home of the president and his wife

The new First Lady, the youngest in the nation's history, brought an added sense of liveliness and refinement to the White House. "The White House under its young mistress will now be the scene of charming festivities," *Harper's Weekly* magazine correctly predicted. At public receptions thousands of curious ladies crowded close to shake the hand or get a glimpse of their gracious hostess. In time the newlyweds grew tired of all the publicity. To escape the eyes of prying newspapermen they often retreated to Oak View, a handsome summer home Cleveland bought in Georgetown, just outside of Washington.

As a happily married man, Cleveland wished to please his wife in any way he could. The rough manners of his bachelor days disappeared. He took care of his appearance and played his role in social affairs with bright and cheerful courtesy. Still, he performed his duties as president with a level head, honest hard work, and dignity.

Opposite page: Mrs. Cleveland, 1886

Grover Cleveland
dedicates the
Statue of Liberty,
October 28, 1886.

On October 28, 1886, Cleveland presided at an important celebration in New York Harbor. On Bedloe's Island, workmen unveiled the great 151-foot bronze Statue of Liberty, a gift from the people of France. Spectators cheered themselves hoarse and scores of tugboat whistles loudly blew at the sight of this grand new emblem of American freedom. In Washington Cleveland also gladly signed a law creating the Interstate Commerce Commission (ICC) in 1887. The nation's first federal regulatory agency, the ICC made sure interstate railroads charged fair transportation rates. Among other national business, Cleveland welcomed the creation of the U.S. Department of Agriculture in February 1889 to look out for the welfare of America's farmers.

Cleveland's greatest impact during his term, however, remained his constant courage in turning down wasteful, unjust bills. Many northern veterans of the Civil War wished to obtain government pensions for injuries they claimed were connected with their military service. These veterans persuaded their congressmen to sponsor hundreds of separate pension bills in their behalf. Cleveland signed many of these bills. Others, however, were obviously dishonest. One veteran placed a claim for military benefits after breaking his leg falling into a cellar. Another hoped to collect money after being thrown from a buggy. The powerful Grand Army of the Republic, the North's Civil War veterans' organization, howled when Cleveland began vetoing these and other equally ridiculous bills. The president, though, refused to budge. "Though the people support the Government," he boldly insisted, "the Government should not support the people."

During his four-year term Cleveland issued more than 300 veto messages. From George Washington to Chester A. Arthur, the previous twenty-one presidents had issued a total of only 132 vetos. Many Americans, however, admired the president's tough stand. It seemed Grover Cleveland had made a successful career for himself simply by saying no. The "Veto Governor" had become the "Veto President," and soon on playgrounds across the country children could be heard singing:

> "A fat man once sat in a President's chair,
>   singing Ve-to, Ve-to,
> With never a thought of trouble or care,
>   singing Ve-to, Ve-to."

Chapter 5

The Years Between

"My God, what is there in this office that any man should ever want to get into it!" complained Cleveland during his term as president. Office-seekers still bothered him every day. The Grand Army of the Republic attacked him for his veto policies. Thirsting after gossip about their marriage, newspapermen refused to grant the president and First Lady a moment's peace. Only Cleveland's honest sense of duty to the country made him willing to run for a second term.

In June of 1888, the Democratic national convention convened in Saint Louis. As bands blared and delegates waved banners, the convention unanimously nominated Cleveland to run again. When the Republicans met at their convention in Chicago a few days later, they balloted seven times before choosing their candidate. Finally they picked ex-senator Benjamin Harrison of Indiana. A Union veteran of the Civil War, General Harrison was the grandson of ninth U.S. president William Henry Harrison.

Daniel Dougherty nominates Cleveland at the 1888 Democratic national convention.

As the 1888 political race got under way, Republican party managers amassed hundreds of thousands of dollars in campaign contributions. The Republicans spent money on noisy parades, public meetings, and piles of political pamphlets. At some rallies Republicans attacked Cleveland's personal character. They called him the "Beast of Buffalo" and claimed that he got drunk in the White House and even beat his young wife. In response to these ugly rumors, Frances Cleveland finally issued a public statement praising her husband as "kind, considerate and affectionate." She wished other wives could only be as happy as she was.

A campaign poster for the Democratic presidential campaign of 1888. Grover Cleveland was the presidential candidate and Allen G. Thurman of Ohio was the vice-presidential candidate. In the center is Cleveland's popular wife, Frances.

The great issue of the campaign was the tariff. From his home in Indianapolis, Harrison gave front-porch speeches insisting the high tariff should be protected. Marching in parades, Republicans chanted, "No, no, no free trade!" For his part Cleveland remained at work in the White House and failed to campaign actively. Other Democrats made weak and fitful efforts to show that a lower tariff would promote competition and help the economy by lowering the price of consumer goods.

A cartoon on the heated 1888 presidential election campaign

On November 6 Americans made their final choices in another extremely close election. At the White House Cleveland waited patiently as voting results were telegraphed. Shortly after midnight the tallied figures revealed:

	Popular Vote	Electoral Vote
Grover Cleveland	5,540,329	168
Benjamin Harrison	5,439,853	233

Cleveland had actually polled over 100,000 more popular votes than Harrison. According to the Constitution, though, it was the electoral votes of the states that determined the winner, and Harrison carried the majority. The Indiana politician had won the election fairly.

Cleveland accepted his defeat calmly and almost with relief. As he prepared to return to private life early in March 1889, he claimed that there was "no happier man in the United States." Frances Cleveland packed her bags on inauguration day with a different attitude. To one White House servant she instructed, "Now Jerry, I want you to take good care of all the furniture and ornaments in the house, and not let any of them get lost or broken, for I want to find everything just as it is now, when we come back again." With surprise the servant asked when she expected that to be. "We are coming back just four years from today," replied Mrs. Cleveland confidently.

The Clevelands moved to New York City and the ex-president joined a well-known law firm. Each day he walked to the office and carefully attended to legal business, just as he had as a young lawyer. On October 3, 1891, a personal event brought added joy into Cleveland's life. "A few minutes after midnight," Cleveland wrote a friend, "a little strong, healthy girl arrived at our home." All America fell in love with Baby Ruth Cleveland and newspapers followed her progress closely.

During long vacations the Clevelands relaxed at Gray Gables, a rambling summer house Cleveland bought at Buzzards Bay on the Massachusetts coast. The neighborhood abounded with streams and ponds, and fishing remained by far the ex-president's favorite pastime. One day he boarded a boat with friends. "All day long on Buzzards Bay we sailed and fished," he revealed. "The wind was blowing freshly and the boat bounded over the waves for twenty miles or more down the bay."

During President Harrison's term of office many things occurred that made Cleveland angry. In 1890 the Republican-controlled Congress passed a new tariff. The McKinley Tariff (named for its sponsor, future president William McKinley) taxed many import items at rates higher than ever before. The Congress also granted higher pensions for northern Civil War veterans, and encouraged the wider use of silver coins, therefore weakening the value of the nation's gold supply. When Cleveland left office the vaults of the U.S. Treasury were swollen with a huge surplus. Congress at the end of Harrison's term had spent so much money on wasteful projects it became known as the "Billion Dollar Congress," and it left the treasury almost empty.

Predicting national disaster if things continued, Cleveland agreed to run for president again in 1892. The crooked politicians of New York's Tammany Hall tried to prevent Cleveland's renomination, but most delegates at the 1892 Democratic national convention in Chicago clamored for Cleveland's return. On the first ballot they picked Cleveland for their presidential candidate and later chose former Illinois congressman Adlai E. Stevenson to run for vice-president.

The Republicans rallied around President Harrison again at their convention in Minneapolis. As the election race began, a third political party rose up in the rural South and West. Many farmers facing economic hardship found the policies of both Cleveland and Harrison unacceptable. Calling themselves the Populist party, they nominated Iowa lawyer James B. Weaver for president.

DEMOCRATIC PLATFORM and PRESIDENTIAL NOMINEES.

Above: An 1892 Democratic campaign poster.   Below: The "notification meeting"
for Cleveland's nomination in Madison Square Garden, New York City

Compared with Cleveland's earlier presidential campaigns, the 1892 election proved very dull. In October, First Lady Caroline Harrison died, and while President Harrison mourned, Cleveland respectfully stopped campaigning. Although Populist party members excited listeners with rousing speeches calling for justice for farmers, the party was actually too small to influence the election greatly.

On election night Cleveland sat at Gray Gables while a special telegraph wire clicked voting results. Friends and family carefully tabulated the incoming numbers and tried to make predictions. Suddenly Cleveland rose from his chair. "I forgot to dry my lines today," he remembered. More interested in his fishing than in the presidential election, he calmly walked outside to hang his fishing lines out to dry. Not until dawn the next day did Cleveland learn that he had been reelected president, the first and only candidate ever to win two nonconsecutive terms. The vote totals finally revealed:

	Popular Vote	Electoral Vote
Grover Cleveland	5,556,918	277
Benjamin Harrison	5,176,108	145
James B. Weaver	1,041,028	22

The spendthrift Republican administration had been turned out of office. In cities and towns thrilled Democrats celebrated Cleveland's victory by singing:

"Grover! Grover! Four more years of Grover!
Out they go, in we go; then we'll be in clover!"

Above: Cleveland's inaugural procession in Washington, D.C., in 1893
Below: President Cleveland (right) and Vice-President Stevenson (left)

Chapter 6

The Second Term

Just as his wife had predicted, Grover Cleveland returned to the White House in 1893. A fierce snowstorm pelted the crowd huddled at the Capitol to witness the inauguration on March 4. As Cleveland took the oath of office and delivered his brief address, surely he knew the nation stood on the brink of financial ruin.

Four years of careless Republican spending and unsound policies were pushing America into its worst depression ever. Unable to survive in uncertain times, factories and railroads were suddenly going bankrupt. The prices of farm products were falling. Frightened businessmen were firing employees and cutting back production. Enraged laborers rioted in Chicago, and on New York's Wall Street panicky investors rushed to sell their stocks.

Soon after taking office Cleveland realized the need for drastic action. Gold reserves in the national treasury had dropped to a dangerous level. The president blamed this drain on the increased minting of silver coins allowed by the Sherman Silver Purchase Act. Demanding that the law be repealed, Cleveland called for Congress to meet in special session in August.

The days of spring and summer passed in a torrent of national restlessness and worry. Millions of Americans suddenly depended upon Cleveland's leadership. Certainly fear would have swept across the country if they had known that the president was gravely ill. On the night of June 30, 1893, a large, heavy man with a bushy mustache secretly climbed aboard Commodore Elias C. Benedict's yacht *Oneida* in New York Bay. Below deck doctors made hurried preparations for surgery. The next day as the boat steamed across Long Island Sound President Cleveland submitted to the dangerous operation to remove the cancer from his mouth. Before the *Oneida* docked at Cleveland's home in Buzzards Bay, doctors had removed his entire upper left jawbone. Through many days of painful recovery the tough president never complained. Instead he concentrated on the upcoming fight to repeal the Sherman Silver Purchase Act.

Cleveland's operation and new rubber jaw remained a total secret as he returned to Washington. Leading the battle with arguments from the White House, Cleveland witnessed the final overturning of the Silver Act on October 30, 1893, by a Senate vote of 48 to 37. The *Washington Post* declared, "The outcome of the fight is a great personal victory for President Cleveland." If Americans had known of his courageous triumph over cancer at the same time, they would have been doubly impressed.

Cleveland's health improved and the repeal of the Sherman Silver Purchase Act restored confidence in the American dollar. The national depression, however, continued into 1894. As hundreds of banks failed and

American business is shown drowning in a sea of silver coins.

unemployment lists grew longer, Cleveland sought other ways to help the economy. One day a reporter asked if the president planned to revise the tariff. "What were we elected for?" loudly responded Cleveland. "What were we elected for?"

Cleveland pushed hard for tariff reform. In August 1894 the Wilson-Gorman Act reached his desk. This reform bill failed to lower tariffs as much as Cleveland wanted. It was better than nothing, however, and he allowed it to become law. Democrat Wayne MacVeagh comforted Cleveland with words of cheer. "Now for the first time in an entire generation—since 1861—you have turned a revision of the tariff away from higher to lower duties. For the first time in that long period trade is to be freer and the people's burdens less heavy."

In spite of Cleveland's efforts, the national depression worsened. Upheaval seemed to rule the land as workmen struggled to protect their jobs and improve their lives. Paid only six dollars a week, striking textile workers picketed at New England factory gates. Steelworkers marched out of mills in Pennsylvania, and over 100,000 coal miners dropped their picks and shovels and demanded better treatment in Colorado. Across the country violence flared as factory owners and police deputies tried to break up these union strikes.

At Massillon, Ohio, bands of ragged, hungry men gathered in the spring of 1894. Led by "General" Jacob S. Coxey, this growing crowd called for government action to create jobs. "Coxey's Army" of as many as 25,000 men set out on a march to Washington to voice their demands. Day after day the army tramped along, yelling and terrorizing the countryside. Many hungry and discouraged marchers, however, quit along the way. In May Coxey reached Washington with only about four hundred supporters. The district police beat and chased off most of these men. The rebellious protest ended as police hauled Jacob Coxey away to jail for trespassing on the Capitol lawn.

The Pullman strike that loomed up soon afterwards posed an even greater threat to national peace. When millionaire George Pullman sharply reduced wages at the Pullman Palace Car Company in Chicago, angry workers went on strike. They refused to build his railroad cars under such unfair conditions. Eugene V. Debs, leader of the American Railway Union, urged his members to join the strike in sympathy.

Right: Steelworkers in Homestead, Pennsylvania, stage a riot in 1892 in which ten men are killed.

Below: "General" Coxey and his army are escorted from the Capitol during his protest march on Washington, D.C.

Above: Federal
troops escort a train
through jeering, fist-
shaking workmen in
Chicago during the
Pullman strike
of 1894.

Left: Eugene Debs,
leader of the
American Railway
Union, who urged his
union members to
strike in sympathy
with the Pullman
strikers

In June 1894 from coast to coast thousands of train engineers, conductors, and trackmen stopped their railroad work. In Chicago and other cities, striking crowds blocked the tracks and refused to let locomotives pulling Pullman cars pass. Debs insisted that the strikers protest peacefully. Nevertheless, banner headlines in the *Chicago Tribune* blared what was closer to the truth: "MOB IS IN CONTROL! LAW IS TRAMPLED ON."

U.S. Attorney General Richard Olney was a friend of the railroad owners. He claimed strikers were preventing the movement of railroad cars carrying U.S. mail through Chicago.

President Cleveland believed him. Through legal channels he ordered the breakup of the strike. To stop the violence in Chicago he ordered federal troops into that city on July 1.

"If it takes the entire army and navy of the United States to deliver a postal card in Chicago," Cleveland roughly remarked, "that card will be delivered."

Within days riots broke out in Chicago. Strikers with rocks and sticks battled with police. Looters broke into railroad cars, stealing food and setting fires. Frightened soldiers fired into crowds, causing greater panic. By July 8 the rioting finally ended, but twelve Chicagoans had been killed and hundreds more had been injured. Union leader Debs was held responsible and arrested. Everyone knew the strike was finished as railroadmen unhappily returned to work.

The cost to end the bitter Pullman strike, however, had been very high.

Above: Queen Liliuokalani of Hawaii.   Below: An 1895 cartoon suggesting that Cleveland should have been acting faster to enforce the Monroe Doctrine

While economic troubles shook the United States, President Cleveland also had to turn his attention to foreign affairs. Far off in the Pacific Ocean, American merchants and plantation owners wished to gain complete economic control of the Hawaiian Islands. Early in 1893 they staged a revolt and overthrew native queen Liliuokalani. Now with landowner Sanford B. Dole as president, these Americans asked the United States to annex the islands.

Cleveland realized most Hawaiians did not support Dole. He refused to recognize Dole's government and he firmly put an end to treaty negotiations. Many Americans wished to see the United States gain more territory, but due to Cleveland's sense of moral justice the Hawaiian Islands would not be annexed as U.S. territory until 1898. He did, however, welcome Utah as the forty-fifth state in 1896.

In 1895 a U.S. dispute with Great Britain almost led to war. For years the British territory of Guiana in South America had argued with the neighboring country of Venezuela over their common boundary line. Angry at Britain's obvious attempt to grab more land, Cleveland prepared to enforce the famous Monroe Doctrine. Announced by President James Monroe in 1823, the doctrine guaranteed U.S. protection to countries in the Western Hemisphere from encroaching European powers. Cleveland insisted Britain accept the decision of an impartial commission in settling the boundary dispute. If Britain tried to take more land than it deserved, Cleveland warned, "it will . . . be the duty of the United States to resist by every means in its power." Rather than risk war the British finally agreed to the commission's decision.

Mrs. Cleveland with daughters Ruth (left) and Esther (right).
Esther was the only presidential baby to be born in the White House.

Above: Mrs. Cleveland
poses with the cabinet
members' wives

Right: Mrs. Cleveland in
the 1940s. The situation
depicted in the photo
is unknown.

Chapter 7

Princeton Retirement

"No President," exclaimed the Indianapolis *Sentinel* in June 1896, "was ever so persistently and malignantly lied about as Grover Cleveland has been." As the depression raged into 1896, Cleveland became hated across the country. Although he honestly did his best to help the economy, jobless Americans, striking laborers, and political enemies all blamed him for the country's troubles.

Even the Democrats turned against their hardworking leader. Speaking at the 1896 Democratic national convention, South Carolina senator Ben Tillman roared, "We denounce the Administration of President Cleveland as undemocratic and tyrannical." Democrats from the South and West demanded wider circulation of silver. Attacking the nation's gold standard in a spellbinding speech, Nebraska congressman William Jennings Bryan proclaimed, "You shall not press down upon the brow of labor this crown of thorns—you shall not crucify mankind upon a cross of gold!" The Democrats quickly abandoned Cleveland and his policies and nominated Bryan to run for president. Cleveland refused to support Bryan and took no part in the fall election campaign. Although Bryan stumped the country giving fiery speeches, in November voters elected Republican William McKinley.

**Opposite page: Grover Cleveland
after his presidency**

Fifty-nine-year-old Cleveland felt disgraced as he finished his presidential term. On March 4, 1897, he watched McKinley's inauguration and with a sense of relief prepared to leave Washington forever. Within days the Clevelands traveled to the lovely town of Princeton, New Jersey, where Cleveland had decided to retire. Not far from the campus of Princeton University, they settled into a handsome house called Westland.

Cleveland greatly enjoyed the peaceful, comfortable atmosphere of Princeton. He rose early each day, read the newspapers, and answered letters. Sometimes he hunted rabbit in the woods outside Princeton or fished on the Millstone River. On other days he helped his children into the saddle when they took pony rides.

The Cleveland family kept growing until five children romped about the house. Little Esther Cleveland had been born in 1893, the first and only child of a president to be born in the White House. Marion had been born in 1895, Richard in 1897, and Francis in 1903. Cleveland's three girls and two boys brought him tremendous joy. In 1904, however, tragedy struck when twelve-year-old Ruth Cleveland contracted diphtheria and died of the disease. It took some time before Cleveland began to get over his eldest daughter's death.

To fill idle hours Cleveland wrote magazine articles on the law and the presidency. In time his national reputation rose again. Americans remembered his toughness and honesty while president and came to admire him for it.

As Cleveland reached his seventy-first birthday his health began to fail. Aching joints and other illnesses kept

Grover Cleveland in 1908, the year of his death

him lying in bed for days at a time. The heavy, robust man, so famous for his strength and energy, soon grew thin and weak. Early on June 24, 1908, family and friends knew the end was near. At 8:40 in the morning Grover Cleveland died in his bed of heart and kidney disease. The last words the ex-president breathed were: "I have tried so hard to do right."

Saddened Americans mourned as his body was buried in Princeton. They no longer blamed him for all the depression troubles of the 1890s. Their most lasting memories were of a courageous, hardworking, and completely honest man who was unafraid to fight crooked politicians. His willingness to say no had earned Cleveland his nickname "Grover the Good," and many fair-minded citizens came to miss the solid, stubborn veto president.

Chronology of American History

(Shaded area covers events in Grover Cleveland's lifetime.)

About A.D. 982 — Eric the Red, born in Norway, reaches Greenland in one of the first European voyages to North America.

About 1000 — Leif Ericson (Eric the Red's son) leads what is thought to be the first European expedition to mainland North America; Leif probably lands in Canada.

1492 — Christopher Columbus, seeking a sea route from Spain to the Far East, discovers the New World.

1497 — John Cabot reaches Canada in the first English voyage to North America.

1513 — Ponce de Léon explores Florida in search of the fabled Fountain of Youth.

1519-1521 — Hernando Cortés of Spain conquers Mexico.

1534 — French explorers led by Jacques Cartier enter the Gulf of St. Lawrence in Canada.

1540 — Spanish explorer Francisco Coronado begins exploring the American Southwest, seeking the riches of the mythical Seven Cities of Cibola.

1565 — St. Augustine, Florida, the first permanent European town in what is now the United States, is founded by the Spanish.

1607 — Jamestown, Virginia, is founded, the first permanent English town in the present-day U.S.

1608 — Frenchman Samuel de Champlain founds the village of Quebec, Canada.

1609 — Henry Hudson explores the eastern coast of present-day U.S. for the Netherlands; the Dutch then claim parts of New York, New Jersey, Delaware, and Connecticut and name the area New Netherland.

1619 — The English colonies' first shipment of black slaves arrives in Jamestown.

1620 — English Pilgrims found Massachusetts' first permanent town at Plymouth.

1621 — Massachusetts Pilgrims and Indians hold the famous first Thanksgiving feast in colonial America.

1623 — Colonization of New Hampshire is begun by the English.

1624 — Colonization of present-day New York State is begun by the Dutch at Fort Orange (Albany).

1625 — The Dutch start building New Amsterdam (now New York City).

1630 — The town of Boston, Massachusetts, is founded by the English Puritans.

1633 — Colonization of Connecticut is begun by the English.

1634 — Colonization of Maryland is begun by the English.

1636 — Harvard, the colonies' first college, is founded in Massachusetts. Rhode Island colonization begins when Englishman Roger Williams founds Providence.

1638 — Delaware colonization begins as Swedes build Fort Christina at present-day Wilmington.

1640 — Stephen Daye of Cambridge, Massachusetts prints *The Bay Psalm Book*, the first English-language book published in what is now the U.S.

1643 — Swedish settlers begin colonizing Pennsylvania.

About 1650 — North Carolina is colonized by Virginia settlers.

1660 — New Jersey colonization is begun by the Dutch at present-day Jersey City.

1670 — South Carolina colonization is begun by the English near Charleston.

1673 — Jacques Marquette and Louis Jolliet explore the upper Mississippi River for France.

1682 — Philadelphia, Pennsylvania, is settled. La Salle explores Mississippi River all the way to its mouth in Louisiana and claims the whole Mississippi Valley for France.

1693 — College of William and Mary is founded in Williamsburg, Virginia.

1700 — Colonial population is about 250,000.

1703 — Benjamin Franklin is born in Boston.

1732 — George Washington, first president of the U.S., is born in Westmoreland County, Virginia.

1733 — James Oglethorpe founds Savannah, Georgia; Georgia is established as the thirteenth colony.

1735 — John Adams, second president of the U.S., is born in Braintree, Massachusetts.

1737 — William Byrd founds Richmond, Virginia.

1738 — British troops are sent to Georgia over border dispute with Spain.

1739 — Black insurrection takes place in South Carolina.

1740 — English Parliament passes act allowing naturalization of immigrants to American colonies after seven-year residence.

1743 — Thomas Jefferson is born in Albemarle County, Virginia. Benjamin Franklin retires at age thirty-seven to devote himself to scientific inquiries and public service.

1744 — King George's War begins; France joins war effort against England.

1745 — During King George's War, France raids settlements in Maine and New York.

1747 — Classes begin at Princeton College in New Jersey.

1748 — The Treaty of Aix-la-Chapelle concludes King George's War.

1749 — Parliament legally recognizes slavery in colonies and the inauguration of the plantation system in the South. George Washington becomes the surveyor for Culpepper County in Virginia.

1750 — Thomas Walker passes through and names Cumberland Gap on his way toward Kentucky region. Colonial population is about 1,200,000.

1751 — James Madison, fourth president of the U.S., is born in Port Conway, Virginia. English Parliament passes Currency Act, banning New England colonies from issuing paper money. George Washington travels to Barbados.

1752 — Pennsylvania Hospital, the first general hospital in the colonies, is founded in Philadelphia. Benjamin Franklin uses a kite in a thunderstorm to demonstrate that lightning is a form of electricity.

1753 — George Washington delivers command that the French withdraw from the Ohio River Valley; French disregard the demand. Colonial population is about 1,328,000.

1754 — French and Indian War begins (extends to Europe as the Seven Years' War). Washington surrenders at Fort Necessity.

1755 — French and Indians ambush Braddock. Washington becomes commander of Virginia troops.

1756 — England declares war on France.

1758 — James Monroe, fifth president of the U.S., is born in Westmoreland County, Virginia.

1759 — Cherokee Indian war begins in southern colonies; hostilities extend to 1761. George Washington marries Martha Dandridge Custis.

1760 — George III becomes king of England. Colonial population is about 1,600,000.

1762 — England declares war on Spain.

1763 — Treaty of Paris concludes the French and Indian War and the Seven Years' War. England gains Canada and most other French lands east of the Mississippi River.

1764 — British pass the Sugar Act to gain tax money from the colonists. The issue of taxation without representation is first introduced in Boston. John Adams marries Abigail Smith.

1765 — Stamp Act goes into effect in the colonies. Business virtually stops as almost all colonists refuse to use the stamps.

1766 — British repeal the Stamp Act.

1767—John Quincy Adams, sixth president of the U.S. and son of second president John Adams, is born in Braintree, Massachusetts. Andrew Jackson, seventh president of the U.S., is born in Waxhaw settlement, South Carolina.

1769—Daniel Boone sights the Kentucky Territory.

1770—In the Boston Massacre, British soldiers kill five colonists and injure six. Townshend Acts are repealed, thus eliminating all duties on imports to the colonies except tea.

1771—Benjamin Franklin begins his autobiography, a work that he will never complete. The North Carolina assembly passes the "Bloody Act," which makes rioters guilty of treason.

1772—Samuel Adams rouses colonists to consider British threats to self-government.

1773—English Parliament passes the Tea Act. Colonists dressed as Mohawk Indians board British tea ships and toss 342 casks of tea into the water in what becomes known as the Boston Tea Party. William Henry Harrison is born in Charles City County, Virginia.

1774—British close the port of Boston to punish the city for the Boston Tea Party. First Continental Congress convenes in Philadelphia.

1775—American Revolution begins with battles of Lexington and Concord, Massachusetts. Second Continental Congress opens in Philadelphia. George Washington becomes commander-in-chief of the Continental army.

1776—Declaration of Independence is adopted on July 4.

1777—Congress adopts the American flag with thirteen stars and thirteen stripes. John Adams is sent to France to negotiate peace treaty.

1778—France declares war against Great Britain and becomes U.S. ally.

1779—British surrender to Americans at Vincennes. Thomas Jefferson is elected governor of Virginia. James Madison is elected to the Continental Congress.

1780—Benedict Arnold, first American traitor, defects to the British.

1781—Articles of Confederation go into effect. Cornwallis surrenders to George Washington at Yorktown, ending the American Revolution.

1782—American commissioners, including John Adams, sign peace treaty with British in Paris. Thomas Jefferson's wife, Martha, dies. Martin Van Buren is born in Kinderhook, New York.

1784—Zachary Taylor is born near Barboursville, Virginia.

1785—Congress adopts the dollar as the unit of currency. John Adams is made minister to Great Britain. Thomas Jefferson is appointed minister to France.

1786—Shays's Rebellion begins in Massachusetts.

1787—Constitutional Convention assembles in Philadelphia, with George Washington presiding; U.S. Constitution is adopted. Delaware, New Jersey, and Pennsylvania become states.

1788—Virginia, South Carolina, New York, Connecticut, New Hampshire, Maryland, and Massachusetts become states. U.S. Constitution is ratified. New York City is declared U.S. capital.

1789—Presidential electors elect George Washington and John Adams as first president and vice-president. Thomas Jefferson is appointed secretary of state. North Carolina becomes a state. French Revolution begins.

1790—Supreme Court meets for the first time. Rhode Island becomes a state. First national census in the U.S. counts 3,929,214 persons. John Tyler is born in Charles City County, Virginia.

1791—Vermont enters the Union. U.S. Bill of Rights, the first ten amendments to the Constitution, goes into effect. District of Columbia is established. James Buchanan is born in Stony Batter, Pennsylvania.

1792—Thomas Paine publishes *The Rights of Man*. Kentucky becomes a state. Two political parties are formed in the U.S., Federalist and Republican. Washington is elected to a second term, with Adams as vice-president.

1793—War between France and Britain begins; U.S. declares neutrality. Eli Whitney invents the cotton gin; cotton production and slave labor increase in the South.

1794—Eleventh Amendment to the Constitution is passed, limiting federal courts' power. "Whiskey Rebellion" in Pennsylvania protests federal whiskey tax. James Madison marries Dolley Payne Todd.

1795—George Washington signs the Jay Treaty with Great Britain. Treaty of San Lorenzo, between U.S. and Spain, settles Florida boundary and gives U.S. right to navigate the Mississippi. James Polk is born near Pineville, North Carolina.

1796—Tennessee enters the Union. Washington gives his Farewell Address, refusing a third presidential term. John Adams is elected president and Thomas Jefferson vice-president.

1797—Adams recommends defense measures against possible war with France. Napoleon Bonaparte and his army march against Austrians in Italy. U.S. population is about 4,900,000.

1798—Washington is named commander-in-chief of the U.S. Army. Department of the Navy is created. Alien and Sedition Acts are passed. Napoleon's troops invade Egypt and Switzerland.

1799—George Washington dies at Mount Vernon, New York. James Monroe is elected governor of Virginia. French Revolution ends. Napoleon becomes ruler of France.

1800—Thomas Jefferson and Aaron Burr tie for president. U.S. capital is moved from Philadelphia to Washington, D.C. The White House is built as presidents' home. Spain returns Louisiana to France. Millard Fillmore is born in Locke, New York.

1801—After thirty-six ballots, House of Representatives elects Thomas Jefferson president, making Burr vice-president. James Madison is named secretary of state.

1802—Congress abolishes excise taxes. U.S. Military Academy is founded at West Point, New York.

1803—Ohio enters the Union. Louisiana Purchase treaty is signed with France, greatly expanding U.S. territory.

1804—Twelfth Amendment to the Constitution rules that president and vice-president be elected separately. Alexander Hamilton is killed by Vice-President Aaron Burr in a duel. Orleans Territory is established. Napoleon crowns himself emperor of France. Franklin Pierce is born in Hillsborough Lower Village, New Hampshire.

1805—Thomas Jefferson begins his second term as president. Lewis and Clark expedition reaches the Pacific Ocean.

1806—Coinage of silver dollars is stopped; resumes in 1836.

1807—Aaron Burr is acquitted in treason trial. Embargo Act closes U.S. ports to trade.

1808—James Madison is elected president. Congress outlaws importing slaves from Africa. Andrew Johnson is born in Raleigh, North Carolina.

1809—Abraham Lincoln is born near Hodgenville, Kentucky.

1810—U.S. population is 7,240,000.

1811—William Henry Harrison defeats Indians at Tippecanoe. Monroe is named secretary of state.

1812 Louisiana becomes a state. U.S. declares war on Britain (War of 1812). James Madison is reelected president. Napoleon invades Russia.

1813—British forces take Fort Niagara and Buffalo, New York.

1814—Francis Scott Key writes "The Star-Spangled Banner." British troops burn much of Washington, D.C., including the White House. Treaty of Ghent ends War of 1812. James Monroe becomes secretary of war.

1815—Napoleon meets his final defeat at Battle of Waterloo.

1816—James Monroe is elected president. Indiana becomes a state.

1817—Mississippi becomes a state. Construction on Erie Canal begins.

1818—Illinois enters the Union. The present thirteen-stripe flag is adopted. Border between U.S. and Canada is agreed upon.

1819—Alabama becomes a state. U.S. purchases Florida from Spain. Thomas Jefferson establishes the University of Virginia.

1820—James Monroe is reelected. In the Missouri Compromise, Maine enters the Union as a free (non-slave) state.

1821—Missouri enters the Union as a slave state. Santa Fe Trail opens the American Southwest. Mexico declares independence from Spain. Napoleon Bonaparte dies.

1822—U.S. recognizes Mexico and Colombia. Liberia in Africa is founded as a home for freed slaves. Ulysses S. Grant is born in Point Pleasant, Ohio. Rutherford B. Hayes is born in Delaware, Ohio.

1823—Monroe Doctrine closes North and South America to European colonizing or invasion.

1824—House of Representatives elects John Quincy Adams president when none of the four candidates wins a majority in national election. Mexico becomes a republic.

1825—Erie Canal is opened. U.S. population is 11,300,000.

1826—Thomas Jefferson and John Adams both die on July 4, the fiftieth anniversary of the Declaration of Independence.

1828—Andrew Jackson is elected president. Tariff of Abominations is passed, cutting imports.

1829—James Madison attends Virginia's constitutional convention. Slavery is abolished in Mexico. Chester A. Arthur is born in Fairfield, Vermont.

1830—Indian Removal Act to resettle Indians west of the Mississippi is approved.

1831—James Monroe dies in New York City. James A. Garfield is born in Orange, Ohio. Cyrus McCormick develops his reaper.

1832—Andrew Jackson, nominated by the new Democratic Party, is reelected president.

1833—Britain abolishes slavery in its colonies. Benjamin Harrison is born in North Bend, Ohio.

1835—Federal government becomes debt-free for the first time.

1836—Martin Van Buren becomes president. Texas wins independence from Mexico. Arkansas joins the Union. James Madison dies at Montpelier, Virginia.

1837—Michigan enters the Union. U.S. population is 15,900,000. Grover Cleveland is born in Caldwell, New Jersey.

1840—William Henry Harrison is elected president.

1841—President Harrison dies in Washington, D.C., one month after inauguration. Vice-President John Tyler succeeds him.

1843—William McKinley is born in Niles, Ohio.

1844—James Knox Polk is elected president. Samuel Morse sends first telegraphic message.

1845—Texas and Florida become states. Potato famine in Ireland causes massive emigration from Ireland to U.S. Andrew Jackson dies near Nashville, Tennessee.

1846—Iowa enters the Union. War with Mexico begins.

1847—U.S. captures Mexico City.

1848—Zachary Taylor becomes president. Treaty of Guadalupe Hidalgo ends Mexico-U.S. war. Wisconsin becomes a state.

1849—James Polk dies in Nashville, Tennessee.

1850—President Taylor dies in Washington, D.C.; Vice-President Millard Fillmore succeeds him. California enters the Union, breaking tie between slave and free states.

1852—Franklin Pierce is elected president.

1853—Gadsden Purchase transfers Mexican territory to U.S.

1854—"War for Bleeding Kansas" is fought between slave and free states.

1855—Czar Nicholas I of Russia dies, succeeded by Alexander II.

1856—James Buchanan is elected president. In Massacre of Potawatomi Creek, Kansas-slavers are murdered by free-staters. Woodrow Wilson is born in Staunton, Pennsylvania.

1857—William Howard Taft is born in Cincinnati, Ohio.

1858—Minnesota enters the Union. Theodore Roosevelt is born in New York City.

1859—Oregon becomes a state.

1860—Abraham Lincoln is elected president; South Carolina secedes from the Union in protest.

1861—Arkansas, Tennessee, North Carolina, and Virginia secede. Kansas enters the Union as a free state. Civil War begins.

1862—Union forces capture Fort Henry, Roanoke Island, Fort Donelson, Jacksonville, and New Orleans; Union armies are defeated at the battles of Bull Run and Fredericksburg. Martin Van Buren dies in Kinderhook, New York. John Tyler dies near Charles City, Virginia.

1863—Lincoln issues Emancipation Proclamation: all slaves held in rebelling territories are declared free. West Virginia becomes a state.

1864—Abraham Lincoln is reelected. Nevada becomes a state.

1865—Lincoln is assassinated in Washington, D.C., and succeeded by Andrew Johnson. U.S. Civil War ends on May 26. Thirteenth Amendment abolishes slavery. Warren G. Harding is born in Blooming Grove, Ohio.

1867—Nebraska becomes a state. U.S. buys Alaska from Russia for $7,200,000. Reconstruction Acts are passed.

1868—President Johnson is impeached for violating Tenure of Office Act, but is acquitted by Senate. Ulysses S. Grant is elected president. Fourteenth Amendment prohibits voting discrimination. James Buchanan dies in Lancaster, Pennsylvania.

1869—Franklin Pierce dies in Concord, New Hampshire.

1870—Fifteenth Amendment gives blacks the right to vote.

1872—Grant is reelected over Horace Greeley. General Amnesty Act pardons ex-Confederates. Calvin Coolidge is born in Plymouth Notch, Vermont.

1874—Millard Fillmore dies in Buffalo, New York. Herbert Hoover is born in West Branch, Iowa.

1875—Andrew Johnson dies in Carter's Station, Tennessee.

1876—Colorado enters the Union. "Custer's last stand": he and his men are massacred by Sioux Indians at Little Big Horn, Montana.

1877—Rutherford B. Hayes is elected president as all disputed votes are awarded to him.

1880—James A. Garfield is elected president.

1881—President Garfield is assassinated and dies in Elberon, New Jersey. Vice-President Chester A. Arthur succeeds him.

1882—U.S. bans Chinese immigration. Franklin D. Roosevelt is born in Hyde Park, New York.

1884—Grover Cleveland is elected president. Harry S. Truman is born in Lamar, Missouri.

1885—Ulysses S. Grant dies in Mount McGregor, New York.

1886—Statue of Liberty is dedicated. Chester A. Arthur dies in New York City.

1888—Benjamin Harrison is elected president.

1889—North Dakota, South Dakota, Washington, and Montana become states.

1890—Dwight D. Eisenhower is born in Denison, Texas. Idaho and Wyoming become states.

1892—Grover Cleveland is elected president.

1893—Rutherford B. Hayes dies in Fremont, Ohio.

1896—William McKinley is elected president. Utah becomes a state.

1898—U.S. declares war on Spain over Cuba.

1900—McKinley is reelected. Boxer Rebellion against foreigners in China begins.

1901—McKinley is assassinated by anarchist Leon Czolgosz in Buffalo, New York; Theodore Roosevelt becomes president. Benjamin Harrison dies in Indianapolis, Indiana.

1902—U.S. acquires perpetual control over Panama Canal.

1903—Alaskan frontier is settled.

1904—Russian-Japanese War breaks out. Theodore Roosevelt wins presidential election.

1905—Treaty of Portsmouth signed, ending Russian-Japanese War.

1906—U.S. troops occupy Cuba.

1907—President Roosevelt bars all Japanese immigration. Oklahoma enters the Union.

1908—William Howard Taft becomes president. Grover Cleveland dies in Princeton, New Jersey. Lyndon B. Johnson is born near Stonewall, Texas.

1909—NAACP is founded under W.E.B. DuBois

1910—China abolishes slavery.

1911—Chinese Revolution begins. Ronald Reagan is born in Tampico, Illinois.

1912—Woodrow Wilson is elected president. Arizona and New Mexico become states.

1913—Federal income tax is introduced in U.S. through the Sixteenth Amendment. Richard Nixon is born in Yorba Linda, California. Gerald Ford is born in Omaha, Nebraska.

1914—World War I begins.

1915—British liner *Lusitania* is sunk by German submarine.

1916—Wilson is reelected president.

1917—U.S. breaks diplomatic relations with Germany. Czar Nicholas of Russia abdicates as revolution begins. U.S. declares war on Austria-Hungary. John F. Kennedy is born in Brookline, Massachusetts.

1918—Wilson proclaims "Fourteen Points" as war aims. On November 11, armistice is signed between Allies and Germany.

1919—Eighteenth Amendment prohibits sale and manufacture of intoxicating liquors. Wilson presides over first League of Nations; wins Nobel Peace Prize. Theodore Roosevelt dies in Oyster Bay, New York.

1920—Nineteenth Amendment (women's suffrage) is passed. Warren Harding is elected president.

1921—Adolf Hitler's stormtroopers begin to terrorize political opponents.

1922—Irish Free State is established. Soviet states form USSR. Benito Mussolini forms Fascist government in Italy.

1923—President Harding dies in San Francisco, California; he is succeeded by Vice-President Calvin Coolidge.

1924—Coolidge is elected president. Woodrow Wilson dies in Washington, D.C. James Carter is born in Plains, Georgia. George Bush is born in Milton, Massachusetts.

1925—Hitler reorganizes Nazi Party and publishes first volume of *Mein Kampf.*

1926—Fascist youth organizations founded in Germany and Italy. Republic of Lebanon proclaimed.

1927—Stalin becomes Soviet dictator. Economic conference in Geneva attended by fifty-two nations.

1928—Herbert Hoover is elected president. U.S. and many other nations sign Kellogg-Briand pacts to outlaw war.

1929—Stock prices in New York crash on "Black Thursday"; the Great Depression begins.

1930—Bank of U.S. and its many branches close (most significant bank failure of the year). William Howard Taft dies in Washington, D.C.

1931—Emigration from U.S. exceeds immigration for first time as Depression deepens.

1932—Franklin D. Roosevelt wins presidential election in a Democratic landslide.

1933—First concentration camps are erected in Germany. U.S. recognizes USSR and resumes trade. Twenty-First Amendment repeals prohibition. Calvin Coolidge dies in Northampton, Massachusetts.

1934—Severe dust storms hit Plains states. President Roosevelt passes U.S. Social Security Act.

1936—Roosevelt is reelected. Spanish Civil War begins. Hitler and Mussolini form Rome-Berlin Axis.

1937—Roosevelt signs Neutrality Act.

1938—Roosevelt sends appeal to Hitler and Mussolini to settle European problems amicably.

1939—Germany takes over Czechoslovakia and invades Poland, starting World War II.

1940 — Roosevelt is reelected for a third term.

1941 — Japan bombs Pearl Harbor, U.S. declares war on Japan. Germany and Italy declare war on U.S.; U.S. then declares war on them.

1942 — Allies agree not to make separate peace treaties with the enemies. U.S. government transfers more than 100,000 Nisei (Japanese-Americans) from west coast to inland concentration camps.

1943 — Allied bombings of Germany begin.

1944 — Roosevelt is reelected for a fourth term. Allied forces invade Normandy on D-Day.

1945 — President Franklin D. Roosevelt dies in Warm Springs, Georgia; Vice-President Harry S. Truman succeeds him. Mussolini is killed; Hitler commits suicide. Germany surrenders. U.S. drops atomic bomb on Hiroshima; Japan surrenders: end of World War II.

1946 — U.N. General Assembly holds its first session in London. Peace conference of twenty-one nations is held in Paris.

1947 — Peace treaties are signed in Paris. "Cold War" is in full swing.

1948 — U.S. passes Marshall Plan Act, providing $17 billion in aid for Europe. U.S. recognizes new nation of Israel. India and Pakistan become free of British rule. Truman is elected president.

1949 — Republic of Eire is proclaimed in Dublin. Russia blocks land route access from Western Germany to Berlin; airlift begins. U.S., France, and Britain agree to merge their zones of occupation in West Germany. Apartheid program begins in South Africa.

1950 — Riots in Johannesburg, South Africa, against apartheid. North Korea invades South Korea. U.N. forces land in South Korea and recapture Seoul.

1951 — Twenty-Second Amendment limits president to two terms.

1952 — Dwight D. Eisenhower resigns as supreme commander in Europe and is elected president.

1953 — Stalin dies; struggle for power in Russia follows. Rosenbergs are executed for espionage.

1954 — U.S. and Japan sign mutual defense agreement.

1955 — Blacks in Montgomery, Alabama, boycott segregated bus lines.

1956 — Eisenhower is reelected president. Soviet troops march into Hungary.

1957 — U.S. agrees to withdraw ground forces from Japan. Russia launches first satellite, *Sputnik*.

1958 — European Common Market comes into being. Fidel Castro begins war against Batista government in Cuba.

1959 — Alaska becomes the forty-ninth state. Hawaii becomes fiftieth state. Castro becomes premier of Cuba. De Gaulle is proclaimed president of the Fifth Republic of France.

1960 — Historic debates between Senator John F. Kennedy and Vice-President Richard Nixon are televised. Kennedy is elected president. Brezhnev becomes president of USSR.

1961 — Berlin Wall is constructed. Kennedy and Khrushchev confer in Vienna. In Bay of Pigs incident, Cubans trained by CIA attempt to overthrow Castro.

1962 — U.S. military council is established in South Vietnam.

1963 — Riots and beatings by police and whites mark civil rights demonstrations in Birmingham, Alabama; 30,000 troops are called out, Martin Luther King, Jr., is arrested. Freedom marchers descend on Washington, D.C., to demonstrate. President Kennedy is assassinated in Dallas, Texas; Vice-President Lyndon B. Johnson is sworn in as president.

1964 — U.S. aircraft bomb North Vietnam. Johnson is elected president. Herbert Hoover dies in New York City.

1965 — U.S. combat troops arrive in South Vietnam.

1966 — Thousands protest U.S. policy in Vietnam. National Guard quells race riots in Chicago.

1967 — Six-Day War between Israel and Arab nations.

1968 — Martin Luther King, Jr., is assassinated in Memphis, Tennessee. Senator Robert Kennedy is assassinated in Los Angeles. Riots and police brutality take place at Democratic National Convention in Chicago. Richard Nixon is elected president. Czechoslovakia is invaded by Soviet troops.

1969—Dwight D. Eisenhower dies in Washington, D.C. Hundreds of thousands of people in several U.S. cities demonstrate against Vietnam War.

1970—Four Vietnam War protesters are killed by National Guardsmen at Kent State University in Ohio.

1971—Twenty-Sixth Amendment allows eighteen-year-olds to vote.

1972—Nixon visits Communist China; is reelected president in near-record landslide. Watergate affair begins when five men are arrested in the Watergate hotel complex in Washington, D.C. Nixon announces resignations of aides Haldeman, Ehrlichman, and Dean and Attorney General Kleindienst as a result of Watergate-related charges. Harry S. Truman dies in Kansas City, Missouri.

1973—Vice-President Spiro Agnew resigns; Gerald Ford is named vice-president. Vietnam peace treaty is formally approved after nineteen months of negotiations. Lyndon B. Johnson dies in San Antonio, Texas.

1974—As a result of Watergate cover-up, impeachment is considered; Nixon resigns and Ford becomes president. Ford pardons Nixon and grants limited amnesty to Vietnam War draft evaders and military deserters.

1975—U.S. civilians are evacuated from Saigon, South Vietnam, as Communist forces complete takeover of South Vietnam.

1976—U.S. celebrates its Bicentennial. James Earl Carter becomes president.

1977—Carter pardons most Vietnam draft evaders, numbering some 10,000.

1980—Ronald Reagan is elected president.

1981—President Reagan is shot in the chest in assassination attempt. Sandra Day O'Connor is appointed first woman justice of the Supreme Court.

1983—U.S. troops invade island of Grenada.

1984—Reagan is reelected president. Democratic candidate Walter Mondale's running mate, Geraldine Ferraro, is the first woman selected for vice-president by a major U.S. political party.

1985—Soviet Communist Party secretary Konstantin Chernenko dies; Mikhail Gorbachev succeeds him. U.S. and Soviet officials discuss arms control in Geneva. Reagan and Gorbachev hold summit conference in Geneva. Racial tensions accelerate in South Africa.

1986—Space shuttle *Challenger* explodes shortly after takeoff; crew of seven dies. U.S. bombs bases in Libya. Corazon Aquino defeats Ferdinand Marcos in Philippine presidential election.

1987—Iraqi missile rips the U.S. frigate *Stark* in the Persian Gulf, killing thirty-seven American sailors. Congress holds hearings to investigate sale of U.S. arms to Iran to finance Nicaraguan *contra* movement.

1988—George Bush is elected president. President Reagan and Soviet leader Gorbachev sign INF treaty, eliminating intermediate nuclear forces. Severe drought sweeps the United States.

1989—East Germany opens Berlin Wall, allowing citizens free exit. Communists lose control of governments in Poland, Rumania, and Czechoslovakia. Chinese troops massacre over 1,000 pro-democracy student demonstrators in Beijing's Tiananmen Square.

Index

Page numbers in boldface type indicate illustrations.

About the Author

Zachary Kent grew up in Little Falls, New Jersey, and received an English degree from St. Lawrence University. Following college he worked at a New York City literary agency for two years and then launched his writing career. To support himself while writing, he has worked as a taxi driver, a shipping clerk, and a house painter. Mr. Kent has had a lifelong interest in American history. Studying the U.S. presidents was his childhood hobby. His collection of presidential items includes books, pictures, and games, as well as several autographed letters.